FOREVER YOUNG

FOREVER YOUNG

PHOTOGRAPHS OF BOB DYLAN

DOUGLAS R. GILBERT

with text by DAVE MARSH

additional research by JOHN MAY introductory note by JOHN SEBASTIAN

DA CAPO PRESS A MEMBER OF THE PERSEUS BOOKS GROUP

Also by Douglas R. Gilbert

C. S. Lewis: Images of His World (with Clyde S. Kilby)
Flannery O'Connor: Images of Grace (with Harold Fickett)

Also by Dave Marsh

Before I Get Old: The Story of The Who
Bruce Springsteen: Two Hearts—The Definitive Biography, 1972–2003
The Heart of Rock & Soul: The 1001 Greatest Singles Ever Made
Louie Louie: The History and Mythology of the World's Most Famous Rock 'n' Roll Song

Photographs copyright © 2005 by Douglas R. Gilbert
Text copyright © 2005 by Dave Marsh
Introductory note copyright © 2005 by John Sebastian

Cataloging-in-Publication data for this book is available from the Library of Congress.
First Da Capo Press edition 2005

ISBN 0-306-81481-1
ISBN-13 978-0-306-81481-5

Published by Da Capo Press
A Member of the Perseus Books Group
www.dacapopress.com

Da Capo Press books are available at special discounts for bulk purchases in the U.S.
by corporations, institutions, and other organizations. For more information, please
contact the Special Markets Department at the Perseus Books Group, 11 Cambridge
Center, Cambridge, MA 02142, or call (800) 255-1514 or (617) 252-5298, or e-mail
special.markets@perseusbooks.com.

1 2 3 4 5 6 7 8 9 — 08 07 06 05

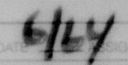 

6/24 B. Dylan No. 10

→2 →2A →3 →3A →4 →4A

→5 →5A →6 →6A →7 →7A →8 →8A

→9 →9A →10 →10A →11 →11A →12 →12A

→13 →13A →14 →14A →15 →15A →16 →16A →17 →17A

→18 →18A →19 →19A →20 →20A →21 →21A →22 →22A

CONTENTS

I SHALL BE FREE—No. 2005

A WORD FROM JOHN SEBASTIAN

This is mainly a thank you to all those involved in these photos. Those few weeks flew by, but they are probably why I felt the confidence to become part of a musical revolution.

My thanks go, of course, to Bob and Sara, Albert and Sally, and the Paturel family for providing that warm, friendly upstairs room that I shared for the sliver of time that I was hanging out in Woodstock.

The places pictured all still look the same. I'm still friends with all the children in these pictures. Woodstock is now my home too.

Thanks to all of them, and thanks to you, Doug, for preserving these moments.

Woodstock, New York
August 2005

Douglas R. Gilbert

PHOTOGRAPHER'S PREFACE

While working as a college intern at *Look Magazine* in the summer of 1963, the thirteen-year-old brother of a friend asked me to listen to a few cuts from *The Freewheelin' Bob Dylan*. I'd never heard of Bob Dylan, but listened. When the boy asked me what I thought, I didn't immediately know how to answer. I'd grown up with '50s rock 'n' roll and had heard some current folk singers, but this was something really different. When I returned to school that September, I took with me a well-played copy of *Freewheelin'* and played it for friends. Most responded with disinterest or were turned off by Dylan's voice and style.

But here was someone who was articulating feeling and impressions and was posing questions similar to my own. I added *The Times They Are A-Changin'* to my collection and I was hooked.

Before my graduation from Michigan State University in March of 1964, I was offered and accepted a staff photographer position with *Look Magazine* in New York. I began working there in April. Staff writers and photographers were encouraged to propose story ideas to the editors, and this was the first story I suggested.

The proposal was accepted, arrangements were made, and the writer and I went to meet Dylan in June. After that initial meeting, the writer left me to work with Dylan on my own. My curiosity to learn who this person was who wrote such compelling words and music was mixed with some initial intimidation. I wasn't sure how he would feel with this stranger who would be shadowing him. It may have helped that he was just a little older than me and was also a Midwesterner.

I had seen some photographs of Dylan singing in a civil rights context in the South. He was in a field with farm workers and some young civil rights workers. This offered a visually exciting setting for photographs of him performing in the rural South at a time when the civil rights movement was a big story. I asked if he had anything similar planned. He answered no. Nothing more than that. But what was initially disappointing proved fortuitous, because I was able to photograph a more private Dylan, surrounded by friends in a familiar environment. I spent time with him at his home in Bearsville, New York, and hung out at the Café Espresso in nearby Woodstock with him and friends. Later, we went to Greenwich Village and then to the Newport Folk Festival.

My way of photographing has always been to be as inconspicuous and unobtrusive as possible—a fly on the wall. I photographed using only existing light and quiet Leica rangefinder cameras. Dylan soon became comfortable with my presence, letting me photograph freely. Once or twice he looked up from what he was doing and asked, "Don't you have enough?"

I think I was with him in the period before he closed himself off from the press and withdrew. I saw some wonderful moments of warmth, humor, and openness. The image of Dylan I held before we met and after my experiences with him was changed. I've thought about that time over the intervening years and see him to be, in some ways, very consistent in spite of his reputation for frequently reinventing himself. He has refused to be fit into categories, either musically or personally. To categorize and label people seems to be a very human need to help us feel that we are in control. If we feel in control we can feel superior, or at least equal. Dylan does not allow us that.

A few weeks later, when the *Look* editors saw the story in its proposed layout they killed it. "He's too scruffy for a family magazine," I was told. Of course I was disappointed and angry with what I thought was a strange and cowardly decision. Over the next two years, my experiences with the way in which many of my stories were presented led me to reconsider my desire to work as a magazine photojournalist. Questions of journalistic integrity, purpose, and the influence of advertisers on editorial content persisted. In time, I stopped working commercially to pursue my artistic vision.

I am very pleased to share this body of work after forty years with the many people who admire and are challenged by Dylan's words and music.

—Douglas R. Gilbert

ACKNOWLEDGMENTS

Thanks to former *Look Magazine* colleague Douglas Kirkland for encouraging me to take this collection of photographs public. Also to my daughter, Rachel (Gilbert) Kokosenski, for enthusiastically pressing me to "do something" with the collection and putting her artist's coach talents to work to help make it happen.

—Douglas R. Gilbert

Thanks to Daniel Wolff, Susan Martinez, Danny Alexander, and John Floyd, each of whom made very valuable comments on this work in progress. Also Lee Ballinger of Rock & Rap Confidential and David Foster of the United Steelworkers Union, who informed me about steelmaking and the Iron Range. Al Kooper was right, as usual. Deep gratitude to John Sebastian, for ably telling this stranger about those days of folk–rock 'n' roll.

I've argued with and learned from Greil Marcus about Dylan (etc.) since 1970. The influence of his writing is all over this book. The influence of Michael Marqusee's *Chimes of Freedom: The Politics of Bob Dylan's Art* was so powerful that I had to suspend reading it or the entire text would have been nothing but a dialogue with his ideas. Thanks to Paul Nelson and Tony Glover for leaving behind such astute and engrossing accounts of Newport, in particular, and Dylan, in general, and to David Gahr, who taught me how to look at Dylan among many other things.

Ben Schafer's editing was a model of extremely helpful grace under pressure.

Barbara Carr and Sasha Carr endured and supported, as by a very fortunate miracle of my existence, they always do. By another miracle, the dogs behaved, especially Coco.

John May's research assistance was invaluable. Sandy Choron took a fleeting comment and helped turn it into a work of beauty, her specialty.

Bob Dylan's songs have been a fascination and inspiration to me since I was fourteen years old. From now on, his work will always fascinate and inspire alongside the photographs of Douglas Gilbert, with whom I am honored to have worked on this project.

—Dave Marsh

The publisher would like to thank Raymond Foye, John Herald, John Sebastian, and Happy Traum for their generous assistance.

I SHALL BE FREE
—No. 2005

I

Bob Dylan stood on the verge of many changes in the early summer of 1964. Though he was in the midst of break-throughs in songwriting and performance, transformations of personal and sartorial style, breakups and new affairs, he hadn't made those breaks yet. He had *not* yet transformed his work or his look; he was not yet Suze Rotolo's, let alone Joan Baez's, ex-boyfriend, or the humiliator of Phil Ochs, or a crony of The Beatles and The Rolling Stones at the top of the pop charts. At the Newport Folk Festival, Dylan was still the biggest star and he still appeared at the topical song workshop because that's where he belonged. In Woodstock, though, he rode his Triumph motorcycle—John Sebastian, just turned twenty and looking innocent enough that he could pass for fifteen, seated behind him—or sat in the town's only coffeehouse for hours, and was never accosted by the public. In Greenwich Village, back in New York City, Dylan and his friends—Sebastian again, and Ramblin' Jack Elliott—still cavorted among themselves in the street, hung out in the Village's many coffeehouses and browsed through its shops without being besieged by fans.

Not much later, Dylan began posing for portraits by the photographer Daniel Kramer, sometimes in settings similar to the photos gathered here. But by then, his cycle of transformation had more visible results. Part of Dylan's breakthrough consists of the image Kramer's photographs define: A slimmer Dylan, with longer hair that seems to have been electrified, and with a complicated look in his eyes—knowing, damaged, stoned, abandoned, thoughtful—that nevertheless seems carefully calculated.

In a proverbial garret, known around town as "The White Room," above the Café Espresso on Tinker Street, he sits down at his portable typewriter and clacks away for the camera.

The Dylan of June and July 1964 caught in Douglas Gilbert's photographs, unseen these past four decades, behaves much more casually. It is not so much that Gilbert's pictures reveal more spontaneity. Dylan was never all that spontaneous when there were people like writers and photographers around. He had come from Minnesota in 1960 bearing a set of composed identities, and in a sense, he spent the next few years mixing elements of each of them. If he told interviewers nothing but fables about his background, remember that every fable contains a substantial component of truth. Dylan's prolific imagination and quick wit made the act of constructing an identity that much more complex.

The photographs of Douglas Gilbert show a Dylan that no other pictures from the period capture. In a proverbial garret, known around town as "The White Room," above the Café Espresso on Tinker Street, he sits down at his portable typewriter and clacks away for the camera. He wasn't bluffing. Gilbert read a little of what had been typed while Dylan was away from the desk. Later, when Dylan's next album, *Another Side of Bob Dylan*, came out, he realized Dylan had been working on the liner notes.

His ability to write for publication while being scrutinized by a photographer isn't all that remarkable—it wouldn't surprise anyone who's ever written in a newspaper city room or, for that matter, who's ever considered that "All the tired horses in the sun / How'm I gonna get any ridin' done," the telling couplet that opens Dylan's 1970 album *Self Portrait*, might be a pun. But no sooner does Dylan get going than he's interrupted—the people who live downstairs, their kids and John Sebastian arrive. Soon, they're all lolling on the bed on the other side of the room, the grinning Dylan not at the group's center but in its midst.

He doesn't look resentful.
He doesn't look relieved.
He doesn't look bored
and he above all doesn't
look distracted. He looks
like a man at his ease in
the world he inhabits.

Dylan, John Sebastian (front center), and the
Paturel clan.

He doesn't look resentful. He doesn't look relieved. He doesn't look bored and he above all doesn't look distracted. He looks like a man at his ease in the world he inhabits.

Which is 180 degrees from how he looks in Kramer's photographs. There, he looks in command, on the cutting edge, ready for any adventure. Here, he's more like Woody Guthrie in that scene from *Bound for Glory*, where the original rambling man confesses: "I been a-lyin' to my own self now for a good long time, sayin' I didn't want no little house and alla that."

Dylan's not lying to himself—in a way, that part about the lying is where he parts company with Woody Guthrie, politically, artistically, and personally. But he doesn't disagree with Woody on the rest of it. He wants this kind of comfort. He wants the other stuff, too—fame, respect, command of his environment and art, no question. Douglas Gilbert's pictures don't change Bob Dylan's history, but they seriously adjust it. These photographs suggest that the family man Dylan became—the one who, according to his son Jakob, "never missed a single Little League game I had. He's collected every home-run ball I ever hit"—had been waiting all along.

Our sense of Dylan in the 1960s is that he lived every day at an extreme—of isolation or socialization, or both. But these pictures suggest that, maybe, instead of describing the young Dylan as purely mercurial, capable of whipping right around from *Blonde on Blonde* to *John Wesley Harding* to *Nashville Skyline*, we ought to see him as someone who was many contradictory things at once: roving bohemian, young folk idealist, rock 'n' roller on the make, poet, jokerman, romantic magpie, attentive lover, budding family man. As complicated as anyone else, maybe more so, but not out of human range.

As his public, we only saw slices of Dylan's life. We saw them consecutively and presumed that all that we didn't see wasn't present. More than that, we assumed that the things that we once saw and no longer could see had disappeared. When the protest songs stopped, so did the involvement with the civil rights movement. (That's clearly untrue.) When the love affair with Baez stopped, the one with Suze Rotolo ended. (Just as clearly wrong.) When he left home, he became a self-indulgent bohemian with no time for quotidian middle-class life, 'til later when he rebelled against the consequences of his fame. (You can't make that case anymore, either.)

We weren't wrong so much as we just didn't have enough information to put it all together. Which Bob Dylan kept saying, not that anyone believed him.

These pictures make me believe him.

II

On the other side of the camera is Douglas Gilbert, twenty-one years old. (Dylan has just turned twenty-three in May). Gilbert already has five years' experience in photojournalism. He sold his first stories to Michigan newspapers while in high school. He just graduated from Michigan State University, and already he's landed a staff job at *Look*, one of America's most important magazines.

To understand the photography-based journalism of *Look* and *Life* in terms of today's photo magazines, you'd have to imagine a blend of *60 Minutes, Time,* and a Sunday newspaper supplement. The photo weeklies covered the world as seriously as any other mainstream journalism of their day. Often, their image-based stories told stories a lot more effectively than anything words could convey. *People* and *Us Weekly* and the rest of the twenty-first century's tawdry crop are as comparable to *Life* or *Look* as a late-model Hyundai is to a Jaguar XKE. When the purpose of newsstand magazines became forcing as much celebrity as possible into every imaginable category, when celebrity—fame, notoriety, the empty vessel of mass recognition without regard to quality—became not just its own but the only category, photojournalism imploded. Just as the Bob Dylan of the middle 1960s would have told you.

From the 1930s to the end of the 1960s, very talented photographers and writers vied for the prestigious staff positions at *Life, Look,* and similar magazines, like *The Saturday Evening Post.* Those jobs paid little, but from them you could forge a career.

In these magazines, a story might emerge from anywhere: Hurricane aftermath; satellite launch; political campaign; plane crash; sit-ins; fashion shows; dog show; late nights in the discotheques.

On the other side of the camera is Douglas Gilbert, twenty-one years old.

They showed movie stars, spectacularly cute kittens rescued from uniquely bizarre circumstances by enormously hand-some firemen, mass murderers, soldiers at war. Celebrity profiles—movie stars, authors, evangelists, political fixers, athletes, folksingers—were part of the mix. But only rarely could naming the star define the story. Elvis's Army haircut was spot news, not the cover story.

Douglas Gilbert's first job threw him, full-grown and innocent, into the apex of this field. *Look* never had the resources that Henry Luce's empire brought to *Life,* but the difference was more in marketing than in quality. Almost everyone had worked their way into these staff positions, arriving from newspapers and freelance work that made the lousy $100 a week seem attractive for its regularity alone. Virtually no one got hired straight out of school.

The job came with a huge expense account. "You stayed in the best hotels, you traveled first class, you ate in the best restaurants," Gilbert remembered. "They wanted to show people that it was a high-class operation. So everyone's goal was to be out on assignment as much as possible."

In a time with only three basic television networks, magazines provided Americans with almost all of their feature journalism. *Life's* coverage of The Beatles on their arrival in America in early 1964 did much to define their image in America—to teenagers and to their parents as well. There was no niche marketing going on; the aim of these maga-zines was to grab every reader who could afford the cover price (a nickel, a dime, a quarter, as years went by) and thus, presumably, the products advertised within.

It took a lot of stories to keep those copies selling and the ads flowing. Everybody's ideas were welcome. Soon after he went to work, his editors asked Douglas Gilbert for story ideas, and he offered them several. One was a profile of Bob Dylan.

The editors knew a little about Dylan, but not much. From their perspective, there wasn't all that much to know. He had enjoyed, which from his perspective was certainly not the right word, a small dose of fame in 1963. In June, Peter, Paul and Mary scored a huge hit with "Blowin' in the Wind," a very emotional but not terribly skillful civil rights anthem whose principal advantage was a luscious melody derived, in part, from the Negro spiritual "No More Auction Block" (also known as "Many Thousands Gone"), a song Dylan had often included in his sets at folk clubs. After that, recording Dylan songs became a trend in the pop-folk world.

By late August, Dylan, previously known exclusively among folkniks, beatniks, and leftists, which is to say Greenwich Village and a half dozen other communities like it, had become enough of a civil rights celebrity to sing from the podium at The Great March on Washington. He did a new song, "Only a Pawn in Their Game," the story of the assassination of Mississippi civil rights leader Medgar Evers, told through the lens of class politics and the canons of white supremacy, which reached his several hundred thousand listeners as a drone. Peter, Paul and Mary did "Blowin' in the Wind." Baez held the trump card: She led the multitude in singing "We Shall Overcome," the movement's anthem.

There stood twenty-two-year-old Bob Dylan, flanked by peers, such as Baez; Peter, Paul and Mary; and Student Nonviolent Coordinating Committee president John Lewis; by idols like Mahalia Jackson, and by legends such as A. Philip Randolph and

By late August, Dylan, previously known exclusively among folkniks, beatniks, and leftists...had become enough of a civil rights celebrity to sing from the podium at The Great March on Washington.

Martin Luther King. At the time, if you'd been willing to bet that forty years later none of these but King would be as well remembered as Bob Dylan, nobody would have taken your money. People might have sneered at the absurdity. Magazine editors, in particular, would have found the idea preposterous, because journalists are in the business of thinking they know how things are going to turn out.

Dylan earned a little more notoriety when a New Jersey high school kid claimed to have been the true author of "Blowin' in the Wind," which did the intended damage. (Although soon revealed as a bratty hoax, the story still floats around the Internet, luring numbskulls to this day.) He not only survived this absurdist controversy, it helped sustain interest in him outside the folk cult.

That September, another Dylan song, "Don't Think Twice (It's All Right)," became a follow-up hit for Peter, Paul and Mary. By mid-1964, Dylan songs had been recorded by everyone from Bobby Darin to The Village Stompers. Sam Cooke did "Blowin' in the Wind" on his *Live at the Copa* album. "Blowin' in the Wind" also inspired Cooke to write his civil rights anthem, the monumental "A Change Is Gonna Come."

Dylan's affair with Joan Baez, the queen of the folk scene, led to frequent appearances at her concerts, which built his audience while spurring a myth that amounted to a Folkie Camelot. Dozens of young writer-performers emerged from the Village to San Francisco Bay, and anyone deemed worthy was dubbed a "new Dylan," a kiss of death exceeded only by "You're no Bob Dylan."

Nor could the British Invasion stop him. The Beatles said they liked Dylan's records (in late August 1964 he'd give them their first joint) and Andrew Loog Oldham took to writing liner notes, like those Dylan did for Baez and himself, for The Rolling Stones albums he produced. Dylan remained less well-known than the British groups but nobody was hipper.

Douglas Gilbert wasn't an especially huge music fan but he liked the popular folk music of the time. In 1962, he talked his way backstage at a Brothers Four concert in East Lansing and wound up shooting the show from the wings.

The Brothers Four typified the popular folk groups that mushroomed in number and popularity after the Kingston Trio kicked off a campus-based folk craze in 1957 with their hit version of the mountain ballad "Tom Dooley." The Brothers Four had formed in 1956 among four "brothers" at the Phi Delta Gamma fraternity at the University of Washington. "Tom Dooley" inspired them to turn pro. They attracted the interest of manager Mort Lewis (later to run the business affairs of Simon and Garfunkel), who got them signed to Columbia Records. Their hit, "Greenfields," a contemporary song that sounded fully traditional, gave them a career—so far it's lasted for fifty years. "The Brothers Four, though disdained in hip folk circles for their frat-house, crew-cut, white-bread style, were and are accomplished musicians, with a knack for recording great songs, old and new," Sean Wilentz notes in his essay about Dylan's 1963 and 2003 appearances at the Newport Folk Festival. (Wilentz also notes that the Brothers Four weren't all that unhip—in 1965, they released a version of "Mr. Tambourine Man" a month before the version by the Byrds launched folk-rock.) The Brothers were not entirely apolitical, but their jibes mainly stuck to showbiz riffing on contemporary topics—dedicating a song to the U.S. troops "...in Mississippi," for instance.

The Beatles, the groups that followed them in the British Invasion, and the arrival of Dylan combined to wipe out the youth end of the market for pop-folk groups. By late 1964, the Brothers Four had been marginalized by everything from their formal attire to their material (which they did not write) to, above all, their harmonies, which lacked blues or R&B accents. Their last chart album, in 1966, was *A Beatles Songbook (The Brothers Four Sing Lennon/McCartney)*, although they retained a live following, especially in Japan. You could tell pretty much the same story about everyone from the Limelighters to the New Christy Minstrels.

But in 1962, when Douglas Gilbert saw that show in East Lansing, the Brothers Four were stars with radio hits and appearances on ABC-TV's show *Hootenanny* (which Dylan and his friends refused to play on, because the producers wouldn't feature Pete Seeger, who was blacklisted for his communist associations).

Gilbert knew how to seize a business opportunity: He sent the group copies of the pictures he made during the concert, and Columbia Records bought nine of them for use on the record package (the inner sleeves holding the actual discs, not the cover) of the group's live album, *The Brothers Four in Person*.

Though the Brothers Four concert was Gilbert's first foray into photographing musicians, it had nothing to do with why Gilbert suggested a story on Dylan to his editors. His reaction to hearing the singer and his songs for the first time led him to that.

During a break from school, Gilbert and his girlfriend visited her roommate in New York. The roommate's thirteen-year-old brother told Douglas that he needed to hear a new folksinger. "So, I listened to him and was not immediately captured or captivated, but I was quite interested in what I heard and thinking that he

needed to be heard more. So, I got my first [Dylan] record not long after that, and began playing it and really got drawn into it."

The Freewheelin' Bob Dylan galvanized many college and high school students, who became the base for Dylan's later transformation into a rock star. Those kids showed good taste. Nothing about *Freewheelin'* was quite normal—the cracked voice, the song lyrics that escaped it, the surreal stories and the lacerating humor in those lyrics. All of it was perfect, from the opening "Blowin' in the Wind," no more jejune than its listeners, to the final "I Shall Be Free," a rambunctious "talking blues" whose title alone stood most of teenage reality on its head, since society continually tells adolescents that freedom is the price of adulthood. "I Shall Be Free," in particular, encapsulates the young Dylan's scabrous politics (the politician in the eighth verse is said to be "eating bullshit") and frankly surreal confessions ("She took off her wheel, took off her bell / Took off her wig, said, 'How do I smell?'") of *The Freewheelin' Bob Dylan* were an aural peek at prospects of ecstasy and delirium that Hugh Hefner's monthly installments of "The *Playboy* Philosophy" only hinted at.*

Douglas Gilbert didn't find his life transformed by listening to *Freewheelin'*. His life had been transformed when he became fascinated with cameras and the pictures he could make with them. But as an artist himself, Gilbert knew he was hearing something special. Something special is what magazine features are (or were) made of. "By the time I graduated in March of 1964, I was really hooked," Gilbert said. "I really liked him; I had memorized

The lyrics to every Bob Dylan song are available at his excellent website, www.bobdylan.com.

Dylan and John Sebastian
35

a lot of the songs. And I knew that I was going to work for *Look Magazine* and thinking it would be really neat if I could talk the magazine into getting me an assignment to photograph this guy, and I'd get to meet him that way."

So, if the story wasn't a priority, a potential Dylan piece certainly made sense to *Look*'s editors. They turned Douglas and writer Sam Castan (who later died in Vietnam) loose on it. Castan was only present for one day of the eight to ten that Douglas Gilbert spent with Dylan.

Dylan's representatives agreed to the shoot, no doubt hoping that a spread in *Look* could do as much to expand public awareness of Bob and his image as the *Life* articles had done for The Beatles. Also, Dylan had recorded his fourth album, to be called *Another Side of Bob Dylan*, in June. Its release was set for the autumn, so from their perspective, Gilbert arrived right on time.

III

The pictures he made tell us what Douglas Gilbert saw when he looked at Bob Dylan in those few days in mid-1964.

What did Bob Dylan see when he looked at Douglas Gilbert?

A young man like himself in some ways, or a young man like he had been not so long before.

Dylan knew Gilbert was from the upper Midwest. He'd have been certain of this as soon as he heard the flat A's of Gilbert's Michigan accent. (We always recognize one another. After I'd been away from Michigan for three decades, a friend's ninety-year-old father, who had left Minnesota sixty odd years before, asked, within five minutes of meeting me, what part of the Great Lakes I was from.)

Holland, Michigan, Gilbert's hometown, is about equidistant from Chicago and Detroit and is so conservative it might as well have been as geographically isolated as Hibbing. Asked if he thought that Dylan recognized in his voice their regional connection, Gilbert said he'd never thought about it, but he wouldn't be surprised if he had. He also allowed that one reason Dylan had come to mean something special to him was "With God on Our Side," which begins: "Oh my name it is nothin' / My age it means less / The country I come from / Is called the Midwest," followed by a summary of American history determined to address and overturn the ideological indoctrination that turned the sons and daughters of the Midwest into almost excessively law-abiding citizens (although often infusing them with a taste for outlawry, too).

It would be futile to argue that Bob Dylan was homesick as late as 1963, when he wrote the songs on *The Times They Are A-Changin'*. But it's pretty clear in those songs that he hadn't gotten his native region out of his heart with *Freewheelin'*'s "Girl from the North Country" and "Bob Dylan's Dream." I suspect that nobody from the heart of America who winds up in New York ever gets completely comfortable with its unknowing parochialism, its lack of both neighborliness and privacy, and its assurance that anyone who's from elsewhere is a hick.

But it's unquestionable that *The Times They Are A-Changin'* is the Dylan album that most directly reflects his Midwestern origins. Though often derided because it contains so many blatant protest songs, it's the first record Bob Dylan made where he began to explicitly explore who he felt himself to be, and not only because of the expressly personal "One Too Many Mornings" and "Restless Farewell." Three songs are written from the perspective of Midwesterners, and those songs ("Hollis Brown," "With God on Our Side," and "North Country Blues") establish the album's weather-beaten mood and battered emotional climate.

"With God on Our Side" is the only one with lines that can be taken for straight autobiography, but all three of the songs work to make the personal political. "With God on Our Side" overturns American war mythology: The wars against Native Americans are presented as genocide, the Spanish-American War as a means of stealing Cuba and the

Philippines and creating a global empire, World War I as without justification except for profit and power. Dylan also scowls at World II's very dubious geopolitical results and the McCarthyist paranoia and nuclear menace of the Cold War. Dylan shows up the social-democratic patriotism often expressed by the new protest singers as the lie it is.

"With God on Our Side" is, perhaps, the one song where the influence of one of his Village mentors, dedicated Trotskyist Dave Van Ronk, shows itself plainly, although there were plenty of other Reds around who shared the same perspective, in New York and before that, in the folk scene in Minneapolis.

Dylan supersedes mere ideology by relating the American story to the Bible. In the last two verses, he invokes Jesus Christ, Judas Iscariot, and the prospect of Hell. The images are from the New Testament but the voice is that of an Old Testament prophet, warning of the consequences of all this unrighteousness.

Religion, of course, is ideology. But in Dylan's writing, religion's function is not to rationalize the inexplicable, especially when one remembers that Dylan has always been in it for the mystery. Religion—or to give his interest its true name, monotheism—plays another role. It promises to deliver on another Dylan obsession: Justice. In this respect, the song's intent would be clearer if it were titled "Without God on Our Side." That's the question it asks: Without God on our side, what makes this supposed trip to the New Jerusalem more than a horror show?

Dylan's love of Biblical imagery blossoms on *Times*. "When the Ship Comes In," a vengeance song written in a snit after a night clerk refused Dylan access to Baez's hotel room because of his appearance, also adopts the prophetic voice from the Old Testament. It careens through every sort of menace he could find

in the Gideon Bible beside the bed. When he sings, "Oh, the fishes will laugh as they swim out of the path," or declares that his foes will "pinch themselves and squeal / And know that it's for real," he's spouting like Jonah landing in Nineveh after the whale. He's rejoicing that these reprobates will never listen to his prophecies and mend their ways. He's got God on his side. Self-righteousness has rarely been so much giddy fun.

But in "With God on Our Side," God becomes an empty vessel. "If God's on our side, he'll stop the next war," Dylan concludes. But the way he sings it unmistakably conveys that God won't stop it—the point is that the task is not God's but humanity's: We're to blame for creating and maintaining all this injustice, no matter who or what we try to lay it off on. Here the streak of religiosity in Dylan's writing comes up hard against his sardonic streak, leaning toward what might be misanthropy (not all that uncommon among monotheists).

This is a Dylan we know very well. It's the Dylan who created the murderous God who kicks off "Highway 61 Revisited" with a suggestion that quickly becomes a threat, one immorally met with only token resistance.

But Dylan has had from the beginning of his career another vision of life, expressed in songs like "Bob Dylan's Dream," "I Want You," "Forever Young," "Every Grain of Sand," and "Emotionally Yours." This alternate center of his work can rarely be seen in pictures of Dylan, for a bunch of reasons, including that hallowed Midwestern idea that some things aren't much of anybody else's business.

The most haunting picture that Douglas Gilbert took shows this Dylan. Dylan sits with his legs folded, yoga-style, next to a little girl, who looks five or six years old. She's the daughter of Bernard and May Lou Paturel, who own the Café Espresso, Dylan's chief Woodstock hangout.

They're in the driveway of the Café Espresso, with a Volkswagen Karmann Ghia behind them and a '51 Ford lurking nearby. Dylan, dressed all in black with a cigarette and sunglasses in his right hand, is just to the little girl's right. She's stuck her legs straight out and her hands fidget. Each of them looks at the camera, straight into the lens, with one eye squinted. If it weren't for that cigarette, you'd be hard pressed to know who's more innocent.

The picture was Dylan's idea. "He took these little kids and they went over and sat on the ground in the driveway. And it was really a beautiful moment," Gilbert remembered.

Gilbert captures the pair just sitting there, not doing anything *but* sitting there (the postures are effortless, as in a lucky snapshot). The Dylan unearthed in this photograph reminds me most of a teenage brother or maybe a very young uncle indulging a kid, while at the same time making a last stab at being a child himself. This is the post-adolescent who became the man who never missed a ball game.

We are decidedly not looking at a misanthrope or even a cynic. Maybe we're looking at a man with those qualities in the bleary face Dylan composes while sitting in Greenwich Village at the Kettle of Fish, with a picture frame hung like a harp rack around his shoulders. ("Take one now," he told Gilbert. "The picture's already framed.") But not here. Dylan "was giving him plenty of time to get into position, not being difficult at all," John Sebastian remembers.

"He took
these little
kids and
they went
over and
sat on the
ground
in the
driveway.
And it was
really
a beautiful
moment."

Dylan with John
Sebastian (on back of
motorcycle), and the
Paturel children, in the
alley behind Café
Espresso.

Not that the cynic wasn't lurking. "There was one incident where, early on, I was a little bit nervous and asking him about or trying to explain what I was doing in a few situations and I remember asking him to do something," Gilbert said. "I can't recall what it was, but I used the phrase, 'I want to make this look real,' that is, as if it's really happening. And, he stopped and looked me in the eye and said, 'Nothing's real, man.' And that had a very sobering effect because I knew what he was talking about."

Douglas didn't stop observing and acting as if some things are real, though, and that's one reason these pictures are different from other Dylan pictures. He was "burning up film," but he also carefully watched for the right things to shoot. "In every situation that I found myself with him, I try to be alert to moments, things that happened either internally with him or between him and another person," Gilbert said. "I guess one of the things that I learned to watch for in any of the photographing was moments of connection, response to another person, to a situation, and to be very alert to what that means, what that meant, what that looked like."

So you can't say that the picture Gilbert made of Dylan and the little girl is real, and the one with the frame from the Kettle of Fish isn't. Nor can you say the opposite. Each is an emotionally accurate portrayal of these people in this moment, which is all that I mean by "true." (Real is another matter. Both nothing and everything go too far. Anyway, as John Sebastian says, "The put-on thing was still remarkably fresh," and if you doubt Dylan's status as the all-time master of the put-on, rent *Don't Look Back,* or just try to figure out one of his interviews, then or now.)

"Take one now. The picture's already framed."

The look in Dylan's face in that driveway picture links to the thread in Dylan's work that allowed him to claim, straight-faced, that all his songs end by saying "Good luck—I hope you make it." ("All" is a stretch—"When the Ship Comes In" and "Positively Fourth Street" pretty much explicitly end by saying, "I hope you squirm for eternity.")

We don't see this Dylan much because professional photography rarely takes place under conditions that will bring it forward. It certainly didn't hurt that he was being shot by a knowledgeable Dylan admirer who knew how to behave professionally.

"I think what happened was that after we got started, he was, in his own way, taking note of how I was operating," Gilbert said. "I think he recognized I wasn't out to do him harm, and that I was respecting him and wanted to get good photographs that would respect him."

Part of the job of any journalist, especially a photojournalist, is raising the comfort level of the subject, not so the subject can be "betrayed" but so the subject can show more of himself. When you're feeling the way Dylan looks here, you're vulnerable, in some of the same ways a six-year-old is vulnerable.

This part of Bob Dylan's spirit animated two of the bleakest songs he or anyone else ever wrote, "Hollis Brown" and "North Country Blues." They are far and away the darkest songs on *The Times They Are A-Changin'*, which also contains a song about a woman murdered by a man "who just happened to be feelin' that way without warnin'." What happens in these songs is worse than that. Worse, in part, because it's much more common.

You could describe "Hollis Brown" as based on a kind of drone—a minor chord played on acoustic guitar serves as its sole instrumental riff, just that chord, repeating and repeating like the bad conscience in a Poe story or, to be more specific, the ticking of the bomb in Hollis Brown's mind as he tries to figure a way to end his indebtedness and move his family to a safer place than their farm on the frozen South Dakota plain. But a riff implies mobility or at least agitation. Neither exists here. Hollis Brown isn't going anywhere. What Dylan's really up to is capturing the monotony of poverty, the excruciating boredom of facing, day after day, the same insolvable economic and social problems, the lack of relief or even variety that defines life lived in such circumstances.

The argument against the song, all such songs, is that they present, as Greil Marcus says of Dylan's protest songs, "social types" rather than fleshed-out individuals. Michael Marqusee makes the case that the fleshed-out individual in Dylan's songs is Dylan, which is true but pretty much displaces the topical aspect of the songs. Anyway, Dylan-as-subject is truer of a straight agit-prop song like "Masters of War" than of a song like "Hollis Brown," even though "Hollis Brown" is no less determined to make its social point.

To me, the mistake is to presume that it takes words to flesh out character. What brings "Hollis Brown" to life as an individual is the music: That guitar chord, in its refusal to cease and its refusal to change; the thudding particularity of the way that Dylan strums it; and most of all, Dylan's barren vocal phrasing. What he sings matters, but how he sings matters more; what the whole thing sounds like matters most. Not all photographs require captions.

It's also pointless to define songs about social types, even if they're given proper names, as worthless or bad art. "John Henry" is a social type. So are Tom Joad, Lot's wife, and the mayor of Casterbridge.

"Hollis Brown" does not rise to that standard, by any means. For one thing, its atmosphere too clearly derives from Woody Guthrie's *Dust Bowl Ballads*, and John Ford's (more than John Steinbeck's) *The Grapes of Wrath*. But that doesn't make it meaningless or even meretricious. The idea that art deserves respect only if it reaches the most sublime status results mainly in hype, as we try to explain why we love things that aren't quite that fine. "Hollis Brown" is more than good enough to make a lasting impression.

In part, that's because of its continuing relevance. By the 1980s, the phenomenon of American farmers committing suicide in the face of insolvable indebtedness had become commonplace, and at the turn of the century, suicide also became a frequent response of destitute farmers in India. Dylan's often booked for lack of sustained political commitment, but his out-of-the-blue plea during the 1985 Live Aid concert to assist the domestic farmer, which begat a series of Farm Aid concerts that lasted more than two decades, reflects a continued concern about farmers in debt—a concern that had the incidental and valuable effect of exploding the central Live Aid fiction, that deadly poverty existed only in Africa and other Elsewheres.

Dylan sings "North Country Blues" in a voice that harkens even more powerfully to the country he comes from. But he sings as someone else, adopting the voice of an aged woman, who recounts the hazards, horrors, and infrequent mixed blessings of her life in a mining town. It's pretty much a soliloquy, the guitar most often faded deeply into the background. The result is so monotonous that the lines "the sad, silent song / Made the hour twice as long" become almost onomatopoetic, but when did Bob Dylan fear monotony? The climax of the song comes when the local mine closes because ore is "much cheaper down in the South American towns / Where the miners work almost for nothing," and the woman realizes "my children will go / As soon as they grow."

Bob Dylan's hometown, Hibbing, Minnesota, stands at the center of the Mesabi Iron Range, the source of the iron ore from which virtually all American steel has been made for a century. Iron mining is Hibbing's only significant industry. When the Oliver Iron Mining Company, a subsidiary of U.S. Steel, discovered that the entire north side of town lived atop a huge seam of ore, Oliver forced the residents to move (not without a struggle). A century later, sidewalks, house foundations, and even streetlights still dot the overlook of Hull-Rust-Mahoning, the largest open-pit iron mine in the world.

"North Country Blues" is only roughly based on what happened on the Mesabi Range. Dylan's high school friend John Bucklen stated Hibbing's problem more completely: "[W]e were aware of course of the economic situation of the iron range at the time, in this town in particular which was sort of hard pressed because of the iron depletion in the mines." New mines in Brazil and Australia took over.

But Hibbing didn't die like the unnamed town in "North Country Blues." Mining revived when new processes made taconite ore, previously considered too inferior to bother with, usable, although of course cycles of industrial stagnation create periodic depressions in the regions that depend on the mines. At the beginning of the twenty-first century, the Mesabi still produced 75 percent of U.S. iron ore.

In any event, "North Country Blues" is more than a protest song against globalization, although it is prescient in that respect. It's also a character study that rises and falls not on how well Dylan conveys the reality of how global capitalism adversely affects people's lives, but on how his singing conveys the woman with her taut, stern, bitter, and sometimes halting inflections. He certainly isn't able to give life to the song the way he does in "The Lonesome Death of Hattie Carroll" (from the same album), the greatest song anyone ever made up from a newspaper clipping. But the whole song builds around the strength of Dylan's careful characterization. Dylan gives the specifics of Hattie Carroll's life in seven lines. That doesn't mean he disrespects Hattie Carroll, any more than the fact that he doesn't give the woman in "North Country Blues" a name means he disrespects her. In "North Country Blues," Dylan brings life to the woman and her town. In "Hattie Carroll," he brings life to the villain—William Zanzinger, an actual person and the very embodiment of a social type—and the situation.

IV

Allen Ginsberg floats through Douglas Gilbert's Woodstock photographs. The picture where Dylan hails him as Ginsberg strolls, hands clasped behind his back, wearing sheer cotton clothes and sandals, catches the famous beatnik somewhere between eminence grise and flat-out phantom. We see the building better in a shot of Dylan wreathed in smoke a few frames later. From this angle, the house looks like it ought to belong to a wizard. Or a poet. (Actually the house belonged to Albert Grossman, Dylan's manager.)

If you make Dylan your focus, it looks more like Bob's just waving to the neighbor who lives in the little house next door. Nobody who's read much Ginsberg (especially "America" and "Supermarket in California") will doubt that he, too, had considered the possibility of a life of such normalcy.

In 1964, Ginsberg was the most famous person in these pictures. Not because of his writing so much: Far more people knew "the answer, my friend, is blowing in the wind" than "I saw the best minds of my generation destroyed by madness, starving hysterical naked," the opening line of Ginsberg's *Howl*. Ginsberg was more famous because he'd become a familiar face in magazines and newspapers and on television talk shows. Allen Ginsberg served as the face of the beatniks, the template of the hippies to come, and the very personification of why Mom didn't hope you'd grow up to be a poet. He also happened to be America's most famous queer (his term).

One poet hails another:
Bob Dylan and Allen
Ginsberg.

Dylan followed by Ginsberg (far right),
and Ginsberg's lover, Peter Orlovsky.

> "You've never
> found your
> kingdom, but
> you've always
> been the king,"
> Bob told him.

Dylan started reading the beats (Ginsberg, Jack Kerouac, Gregory Corso, Lawrence Ferlinghetti) in high school, and he loved *Howl*, the first yawp of the Beat Generation. Ginsberg loved Dylan's songs and look even before they met in February 1964. He understood why turning "Lord Randall" into "A Hard Rain's A-Gonna Fall" mirrored his own effort to modernize the colloquial ambitions of Walt Whitman, in order to create a poetics rooted in American vernacular speech.

So, when they met in February 1964, just after Ginsberg had returned from a long sojourn on the West Coast, they quickly became friends. "Garrulous and inquisitive, Allen could have been the flip side to Dylan's personality," Barry Miles wrote. But opposites can polarize as well as unite. What cemented Dylan and Ginsberg's friendship was their complementary ambitions. Bob wanted to write more like a poet. Ginsberg wanted to use his poetry to make music.

During the Rolling Thunder Revue tour eleven years later, Dylan dragged Ginsberg on the road and dubbed him King of the whole proceedings. "You've never found your kingdom, but you've always been the king," Bob told him. Dylan also understood that for his hairy, ecstasy-seeking (and finding) friend searching for that kingdom—the kingdom of love in all its aspects, carnal and spiritual—was more to the point than finding it.

Over the years, Dylan and Ginsberg planned all sorts of projects. Many were films: A movie based on *Kaddish*, Ginsberg's moving elegy to his late mentally ill mother, Naomi (which was to have been directed by photographer Robert Frank), for instance. They also made demo recordings together in the 1970s. Whatever Ginsberg taught Dylan began long before they met, while Dylan more tangibly taught Ginsberg about music.

Dylan also encouraged Ginsberg to sing, something the poet said he wouldn't have even thought of doing until he heard young Dylan: "His words were so beautiful. The first time I heard them, I wept."

Ginsberg owned a small harmonium, a primitive pump organ, that he acquired in Benares, India. He didn't know how to play it. According to Mitch Myers, in his liner notes to Ginsberg's album, *New York Blues, Rags, Ballads, & Harmonium Songs 1971–1974,* "Dylan showed him the three chords needed to write a folk or blues song, insisting that it was Allen's time to sing out rather than simply reciting his prose." The lesson may have taken place at the table in Albert Grossman's kitchen, where we see the two of them with the harmonium in Gilbert's photographs. Dylan and Ginsberg are conversing across the harmonium but it's Dylan who's sitting in position to play it. Dylan also encouraged Ginsberg to sing, something the poet said he wouldn't have even thought of doing until he heard young Dylan: "His words were so beautiful. The first time I heard them, I wept."

Dylan and Ginsberg's fellowship was intermittent, but it endured through Ginsberg's final illness in 1997. You can't see Allen Ginsberg in Gilbert's shots of Dylan at the typewriter, but Dylan never strayed far from his spirit. That spirit relates back to the vulnerable side of Dylan, for Ginsberg, even at his yowling loudest as in *Howl*, never fully succumbed to bitterness or rage. His subject was love in all its aspects, from sexual passion to compassion for other living things to the lust to unite with the universe. That is the Ginsberg who shows up in Dylan's songs, more than Dylan's periodic usage of Ginsberg-style unstructured and haphazardly punctuated verse, which he mostly reserved for liner notes and other short messages. *Chronicles,* his autobiography, has none of it, but what Bob Dylan learned from Allen Ginsberg is inherent in its entire approach.

Ginsberg and Dylan were passing more than one torch that summer. As Dylan's involvement with political crusades wound

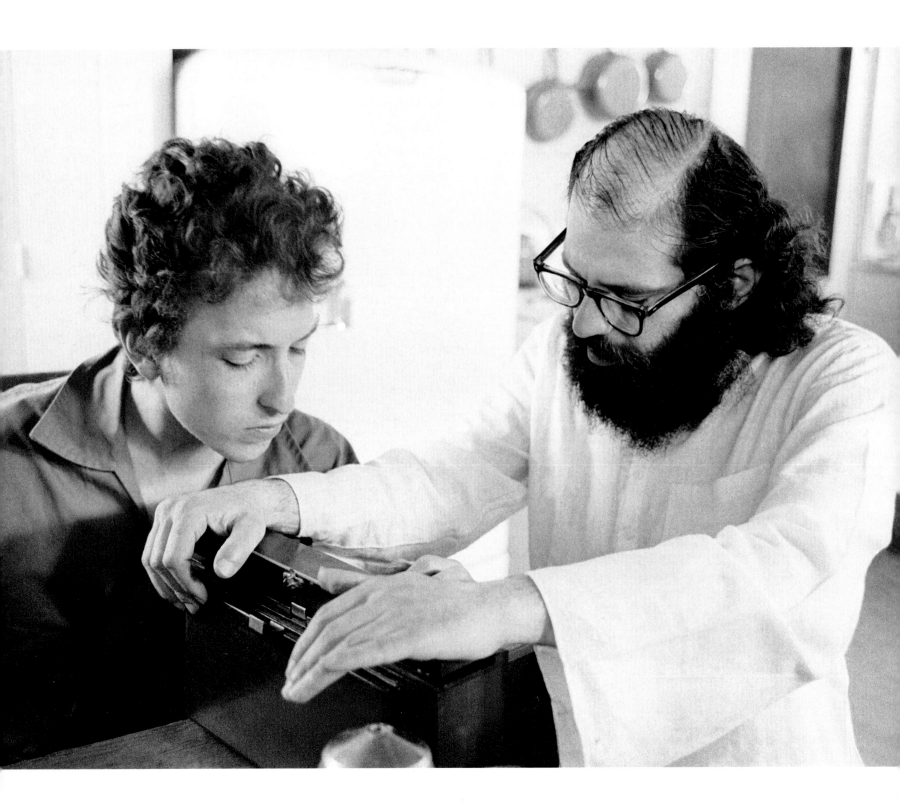

(left to right): Journalist
Al Aronowitz, his son
Myles, Ginsberg, Dylan,
in his manager Albert
Grossman's kitchen.

Dylan, Ginsberg, and Sally Grossman, who was married to Dylan's manager and would later grace the cover of *Bringing It All Back Home*.

down, Ginsberg's intensified. Over the next few months, the poet led the campaign in support of Lenny Bruce and he traveled to both European communist countries and to revolutionary Cuba. Ginsberg never played a role in the civil rights movement—his open homosexuality would have been utterly disruptive; the comparatively closeted Bayard Rustin's created trouble enough—but he was one of the first to join the movement to end the war in Vietnam. Dylan became more aloof from all such large-scale political endeavors, and at least in public, he stayed that way.

V

The presence of Allen Ginsberg in these photographs stands for Dylan's roots in a literary tradition, and his efforts to bond more firmly the literary with the musical.

The presence of John Sebastian stands for Dylan's musical future and his effect on how others write songs and perform them. That's especially true of the pictures made in the Paturel's Café Espresso in Woodstock, where Sebastian plays acoustic guitar and Dylan's on electric bass. (Sebastian would be photographed at the *Bringing It All Back Home* sessions in 1965 with an electric bass. Neither he nor Dylan ever played one much.)

Those pictures don't look like they've captured the opening moments of a revolution but that's just what's going on. That summer, Sebastian looked more like an incipient rock 'n' roller than Dylan did. In particular, his backswept hairdo, which left him resembling Dylan's protest song rival Phil Ochs, harkened to the '50s greaser model. ("We had the Elvis thing going on pretty well," says Sebastian with his usual overdose of mirth.) The guitars remained acoustic. But there's that bass. We don't see the amplifier but the cord trails off to it. Dylan's playing electric, all right, albeit sometimes with the aid of a capo, betraying his guitarist sensibility.

Sebastian, a Greenwich Village native whose father made his living playing classical music on harmonica, began turning up at Village clubs in 1960, when he was only sixteen.

He quickly picked up the harmonica, getting some tips from his father but pursuing folk styles, not classical music. (Sebastian's parents had close friends in the folk music community; John remembered being visited by both Woody Guthrie and Burl Ives in his youth.) By 1962, he began finding work as a studio sideman. In 1964, he was drafted into a casual group of jug band enthusiasts, the Even Dozen Jug Band, whose thirteen members included Sebastian, Maria Muldaur, Steve Katz (later of Blood, Sweat & Tears), guitarist Stefan Grossman, ragtime revivalist Joshua Rifkin, and bluegrass-jazz master David Grisman.

He'd known Dylan practically since Bob came to town. "I was used to seeing him sort of eye to eye in Greenwich Village basements. We were friends because we had a variety of common interests—we were both harmonica players, we were both big fans of Victoria Spivey, things like that." The evidence of that camaraderie jumps out of Douglas Gilbert's shots of Dylan and Sebastian.

In the spring of 1964, Sebastian had "a sort of standing invitation" to run with Dylan, "but I was only able to take advantage of it for a couple of weeks here and there." In June, he and a couple of other friends traveled to Dylan gigs around Boston and Providence, riding in "the famous car" (a station wagon in which Dylan had driven across the United States the previous winter, accompanied by road manager Victor Maymudes and two friends, stopping among other places in North Carolina to visit Carl Sandburg, and in New Orleans, where Dylan wrote the first version of "Mr. Tambourine Man.")

"It was one of those moments when you feel like there are only twelve people in the whole world," says Sebastian, "And we knew everybody."

"It was strictly sidekick space," Sebastian acknowledges. But that didn't bother him—Dylan was the best writer on the scene and a riveting performer. There was a lot to be gained by traveling with him, far more than just hipster credibility (though given that John was three years younger, that too).

It was at those April shows, with Dylan playing so well he literally moved Sebastian to tears, that John first realized the beginning of a change in their relationship. "All of a sudden, this secondary spirit jumped out of him," he remembers with continued amazement. "Things changed really fast." It wasn't alienating—it was simply recognition that transformation was occurring. "I was properly impressed by what Bob was coming up with," he says, deadpan.

Nobody planned John's appearance in the *Look* photographs. Dylan basically lived at Grossman's house in neighboring Bearsville in that period (he had his own room and a separate doorway). Sebastian went to visit him there when he had a chance. They hadn't seen each other in a while because Dylan had spent much of May in Europe, first playing London's Royal Festival Hall, then paying quick visits to Paris and Berlin, and finally some extended time in a house on the Greek coast, where he wrote several of the songs on his next album, most notably "I Don't Believe You."

Sebastian was more than welcome. The Village folk scene remained its own tiny universe. "It was one of those moments when you feel like there are only twelve people in the whole world," says Sebastian. "And we knew everybody."

It wouldn't stay that way long. At the urging of his producer, Tom Wilson, and inspired by The Beatles, Dylan considered using a rock band on his new songs. But Columbia Records pressed him to make a new album quickly in order to feature it at an upcoming

86

sales conference. There wasn't time to arrange and rehearse the songs for a band session. Dylan wound up recording the whole thing in one marathon session on June 9, starting around 7:30 that night and finishing at 1:30 the next morning —an especially amazing feat given that *Another Side* is a very long album, over 50 minutes, which is close to the limit of how much music will fit on a vinyl LP. (The ways in which marketing men determine the course of artistic development in our time will never be fully appreciated.)

Tom Wilson picked the title: *Another Side of Bob Dylan*. Dylan later said he thought it "overstated the obvious," but understated might have been a more accurate assessment.

Even without a band, *Another Side* started a musical revolution. It had no "topical" songs on it, although "I Shall Be Free No. 10," a talking blues, contained a number of topical wisecracks, and "Chimes of Freedom" was an eloquent statement of ethical purpose that honored the bravery of moral commitment. Among other things, *Another Side* recovered Dylan's humorous side, which had virtually disappeared on *The Times They Are A-Changin'*, spat in the eye of the folk establishment from beginning, with "All I Really Want to Do" ("is baby be friends with you"), to end, with "It Ain't Me Babe," whose "No, no, no" was addressed less to The Beatles' "Yeah, yeah, yeah" than to the commissars of the folk music establishment and anyone else who expected to limit Dylan's range as an artist or a person.

He began separating himself from the Folk Police when he made a very controversial (possibly drunken) speech while accepting the Tom Paine Award from the National Emergency Civil Liberties Committee (NECLC). Trouble was brewing when Dylan, who has sometimes seemed uncomfortable making song introductions at his own shows, began, "I haven't got any guitar. I can talk though." He went on to accept the award in the name of the young people who had "gone down to Cuba"—the Venceremos Brigade, who cut sugarcane during that year's harvest to express solidarity with the Revolution, "because they're all young and it's took me a long time to get young and now I consider myself young. And I'm proud of it." It was a summary of "My Back Pages," the song from *Another Side of Bob Dylan,* where he declared "I was so much older then / I'm younger than that now" as a deliberate act of apostasy against righteous liberalism. But that was OK—he even got a laugh when he attacked bald government officials . . . for being bald.

But he moved beyond the comprehension of most of those in the audience (and most of his biographers, too, since few record it), when he said, "There's no black and white, left and right to me anymore; there's only up and down and down is very close to the ground. And I'm trying to go up without thinking about anything trivial such as politics. They has got nothing to do with it. I'm thinking about the general people and when they get hurt." The NECLC was as far left as liberalism got—it was formed during the McCarthy years to defend Communists and alleged Communists that the American Civil Liberties Union wouldn't help—but Dylan's call for class consciousness and his claim that gaining such consciousness trivialized politics stepped over the edge of liberalism.

The situation got worse when he took a swing at the bourgeois Negroes on the platform at the March on Washington, noting of his black friends: "My friends don't have to wear suits. My friends don't have to wear any kind of thing to prove that they're respectable Negroes." He later said he dedicated the award to James Forman and SNCC (Student Nonviolent Coordinating Committee); Forman was known to wear farmer's overalls to posh events.

Finally, he completely overturned the tables by declaring, by way of tribute to his friend Philip Luce, who had led the group to Cuba, "I have to be honest, I just got to be, as I got to admit that the man who shot President Kennedy, Lee Oswald, I don't know exactly where—what he thought he was doing, but I got to admit honestly that I too—I saw some of myself in him. I don't think it would have gone—I don't think it could go that far. But I got to stand up and say I saw things that he felt, in me—not to go that far and shoot." Then the booing began.

The left-liberal community continued erupting after the dinner. Contributions to the NECLC plummeted. Its leader, Corliss Lamont, wrote a formal letter of explanation, in which he defended the selection of Dylan for the award, but not for the speech.

For that, Dylan formally apologized, in his own fashion. He wrote an open letter, which Lamont mailed out with his own:

when I speak of bald heads, I mean bald minds
when I speak of the seashore, I mean the restin shore
I dont know why I mentioned either of them

It's one of the most revealing documents of his career, far more of a confessional than even *Chronicles I,* his great autobiography. For more than 2,000 words, Dylan wrote of how his boyhood in Minnesota had shaped him, and of being reshaped when he came to New York, of what had happened that night, and the predicament he found himself in at the Tom Paine awards dinner. While he hoped that people would understand, he never retreated from saying he had tried to be honest. While the letter urged those offended not to take it out on the NECLC, he also admitted his real mistake:

"I should've remembered
"I am BOB DYLAN an I dont have t speak
I dont have t say nothin if I dont wanna"
but
 I didn't remember"

He never forgot again.

Folk purists believed that popular music was filled with creeping evil, and there were those among them who appointed themselves to police their end of the music world. Even folk veteran Oscar Brand, too genial to qualify as a cop, said, "The electric guitar represented capitalism . . . the people who were selling out." It never crossed such minds that rock 'n' roll might be another kind of voice of opposition.

It even escaped the purists that in such music the poor Southerners, black and white, who the folk movement championed, found in such music a way to speak for themselves. What mattered was not such naked facts but ideology: Electric instruments were bad. People who played them were sellouts. People who stooped to writing love songs, instead of songs about Issues, were on their way to the same Gehenna. It was all as ignorant as Tom Wilson believing, until he heard Dylan, that "folk music was the dumb guys" not sufficiently talented to play jazz.

When asked to discuss the controversy, Dylan brushed it aside. "I mean, they must be pretty rich to go some place and boo," he said at a San Francisco press conference in 1965. "I mean, I couldn't afford it if I was in their shoes."

So when he got bad reviews and snotty open letters and boos from the Folk Police, he never defended or explained. Not, at least, until someone screamed "Judas!" at a Manchester, England, show in 1966. Even then he just said flatly, "You're a liar," and turned to his band. "Play fucking loud!" he commanded. And they did, coming forth with the greatest version of "Like a Rolling Stone" of all time.

But all that was still to come. In June 1964 in Woodstock and the next week at the Kettle of Fish bar back in the Village, the verbal jousting was still sport and the put-on was, indeed, still fresh. The transformation had begun but it wasn't very visible yet. It was audible, but the Folk Police never had very acute hearing.

That electric bass wasn't just lying around for no good reason. Dylan had heard in The Beatles' first American hits expressive possibilities that, when he began playing folk music, he thought rock 'n' roll couldn't possess. (Dylan was a hard-core Little Richard enthusiast and general rock 'n' roll performer all through high school.)

"I should've remembered
"I am BOB DYLAN an I dont have t speak
I dont have t say nothin if I dont wanna"

Younger folkies like John Sebastian could hear Dylan very well. That winter, Sebastian was upstate in an ice-cold off-season hotel he and some friends had rented to rehearse a new group they were forming, when he got a call from Dylan, who offered John a job as electric bassist in the band he was putting together. Sebastian took several deep breaths and said with great regret that he couldn't do that, because he was committed to this other group. Then he went back to rehearse some more, wondering if he'd really just heard himself turning down a chance to play with Bob Dylan for a chance to start a group with Zal Yanovsky. This was four months before Dylan released his first rock single, "Subterranean Homesick Blues," the official starting point in the history of folk-rock.

It worked out well for everyone. By August 1965—fourteen months after the *Look* photo shoots—the Lovin' Spoonful, starring Sebastian and Yanovsky, had a Top Ten single with "Do You Believe in Magic?" It was the first of seven Top Ten hits in a row. By the time the seventh dropped off the charts, Dylan had released the three rock albums—*Bringing It All Back Home, Highway 61 Revisited,* and *Blonde on Blonde*—that made him a legend and a fortune (and a prisoner of fame—he learned to cope). By then, there were dozens, if not hundreds, of folk-rock bands playing electric versions of "Greenfields" and adding sitar to "You're Comin' 'Round the Mountain" and otherwise tormenting the Folk Police.

Douglas Gilbert had no inkling that he was photographing the beginnings of this, but he had a good ear and a good memory. "I wasn't all that surprised," he said of hearing Dylan's electric music a few months later. "I remembered that he'd done 'Corrina Corrina' [a blues standard] with a piano and drums on *Freewheelin'*."

VI

Douglas Gilbert made his first Dylan pictures in Woodstock more as a matter of happenstance than fate. Though the town had long been a haven for artistic and bohemian types, the area was still a retreat, without the resonance the place (or its name) would have in the wake of Dylan's supposed "retirement" there in 1966, and the gigantic rock festival that took over the area in the summer of 1969. The appearance of a *Look* photographer in 1964 Woodstock had no particular contemporaneous feeling of history being made, any more than Dylan aboard the Triumph 750 would inspire foreboding that three summers later Dylan would have the music world's most famous motorcycle accident on the roads nearby.

The town of Woodstock exists at the edge of the world Gilbert portrays. It is seen clearly only in the shot of Dylan and Sebastian aboard the bike, about to turn onto the main drag. (Sebastian says the same buildings are still there, though all the signs have changed.) Café Espresso could be anywhere. The "White Room" above has more distinctive features, as Gilbert shows in both the picture with the family on the bed and the shot of Dylan typing, framed by a smoking table in front of him, an architect's drawing table behind him, and a rack of tools hanging over his head. The rest of the time, Dylan could be almost anywhere, even in the astonishing picture where he sits in a rocking chair watching Dean Martin on a TV that's perched in a bay window. If it didn't say Café Espresso in the window, the group of people, including *Candy* co-author Mason Hoffenberg and Dylan's future wife, Sara Lowndes, sitting at the red-checked table cloth might be anywhere in Sebastian's bohemian world of a dozen people.

Dylan and Dino

(left to right) Unidentified, Sara Lowndes, *Candy* co-author Mason Hoffenberg, John Sebastian, Dylan, and Victor Maymudes, Dylan's roadie and traveling companion.

New York City intrudes itself into a few of the pictures taken there, but mainly that shoot takes place in the world of bohemia, too. Indeed, when Dylan, Ramblin' Jack Elliott, and John Sebastian survey the French LP *Dansez avec les trios grands* while standing around an open car door in the middle of the street, the effect is very much the Left Bank meets the Village. Thumbing through books in a Village shop, Dylan could be anywhere in that orbit, too, and that's true even in the distinctively shabby little barroom of the Kettle of Fish, with its bill of fare hung on a letterboard, its vaguely seedy denizens, and its water glasses half-filled with red wine.

The few pictures of Bob Dylan alone here tell us that this is not the kid from the Mesabi Range. This is Bob Dylan, New Yorker. Greenwich Village, its streets, shops, and taverns are the only home this Dylan needs. It is in its own way a smaller place than Hibbing. The sign as you leave the 14th Street subway station might read, ENTERING GREENWICH VILLAGE, POP. 12.

As Dylan wrote in his NECLC apology:

> I was given my direction from new york. I was fed in
> new york. I was beaten down by new york an I was
> picked up by new york. I was made t keep going on
> by new york...
> like a friend of mine, jack elliott, who says he
> was reborn in Oklahoma, I say I was reborn in
> New York...

This is a Dylan we know quite a lot better than the one captured in the Woodstock pictures. Which is to say, this part of

Sebastian, Dylan, and Ramblin'
Jack Elliott in the Village.

Book browsing in the Village
with Maymudes.

his private life overlaps his public life more closely. There are hundreds of windows overlooking the streets on which he and his friends meet and chat. The whole town's a stage—and yet, it's a stage where not just Dylan but millions of others live their private lives. Maybe to be reborn as a New Yorker is to come to terms with the fact that the potential for a stage is everywhere, that the private comforts of little houses are something of an illusion. You have to be willing to pay the price for the stage as much as you have to pay for the house, but this mortgage is not repaid in money.

Dylan's not famous yet. He's well on his way to developing his enigmatic legend, though, and if Douglas Gilbert's experience is any measure, he'd already earned the enigma part. "I can remember, at times, at the end of a day I would be feeling extremely frustrated. And, in some curious way—didn't like him very much as a person. I never lost the respect for his work, but, just personally, he could be so frustrating that I would find that I was talking to myself about how difficult [the process] was.

"There was a kind of frustration with what I felt I was trying to get at sometimes—with understanding him, where I would think I was beginning to get a little closer insight, and he would turn it around. Or, he would say something, or do something, that I would find confusing or going in a whole other direction. It was like he wasn't letting me all that close at times. It's really hard to describe." Not very hard to believe, for anyone who's followed Dylan closely over the years. It can sometimes seem that the only thing he dislikes more than being misunderstood is being understood.

The Dylan of Greenwich Village still looks pretty clean-cut, close-shaven, neatly if casually dressed. Emotionally, he looks at

peace in his own skin, as he rarely would after he became a rock star. It helps that he's photographed at one of his favorite hangouts, the Kettle of Fish bar in the Village. "It was obviously a place he was very comfortable in. And, as I recall it was an afternoon of red wine," Gilbert said, recalling that when Dylan came up with the idea of being photographed with a picture frame hanging around his neck, "he was fairly loose at that point."

The Dylan Douglas Gilbert's photos reveal isn't the rascal on the cover of *Bringing It All Back Home,* let alone the wraith on *Highway 61 Revisited,* or the stern man who doubtfully welcomes us to *Blonde on Blonde.* In Douglas Gilbert's photos, Dylan's still a young man, almost a kid, enjoying his life and his friends. More than anything, he seems unburdened.

He does not seem, by any stretch of the imagination, what you might call "normal." He doesn't strike us that way now and he would certainly not have seemed normal in 1964.

Sebastian, and even Elliot, often seen as a pretty rough character, look pretty tidy too—for bohemian folksingers. In the shot with the French record albums, Ramblin' Jack appears as a cowboy handsome enough for Marlboro. The Kettle of Fish is a little run-down but that's the nature of a New York City bar, isn't it? Nobody here (or, come to that, in Woodstock) looks like they've slept in their clothes. The men's hair isn't long, though Dylan's *is* beginning to look, as he later described it, as if he'd slept on it for twenty years.

Ramblin' Jack Elliott and Dylan at the Kettle of Fish.

Yet *Look*'s editors eventually rejected the whole Dylan shoot as "too scruffy looking for a family magazine." Gilbert says that the advertising department also had a hand in the decision making but "the editors wouldn't tell us that." In this case, both the editors and the admen might have had the same problem.

What did they see that we don't?

Start with what they did not see. A star, or at least a leading man. A guy who lived in the world where these magazines were intended to go. *Look*'s job was to tell its subscribers what was going on in that world, not that there were parallel universes in which Andy Williams was a nobody and school was out, permanently. Let alone that those worlds were becoming accessible to the impressionable children who would also see this story. *Look*'s own editors didn't look like this. Neither did its writers or photographers. What Douglas Gilbert had found, explored, and come to terms with was not a first-class operation. It was a no-class operation— on purpose. Scruffy is a kind word for the responses most middle-aged men of the 1960s gave to their first glimpses of the mass bohemia aborning.

If the Kettle of Fish had been a bar and grill in Grinnell, Iowa—based on its décor, it could have been—and a presidential campaign had passed through it for an afternoon, maybe those pictures would have made sense. But pictures of a guitar-playing poet with an electroshock hairdo, long sideburns, a black turtle-neck, a suede jacket and metal-frame Ray-Bans in a beatnik bookstore? Scruffy, said the prisoners of their time. And we are all prisoners of our time.

But let's not soft-pedal their side of the story, either: It's one thing to be unable to cope with the future when it first shows its face. Not much blame attaches to it. But Gilbert remembers that

Dylan and Baez had come up to the *Look* offices to look over the story's layout. He found out when he ran into them on the street outside the magazine's office. They were pleased with what they'd seen, and he was pleased they'd seen it.

When he got inside, though, an editor told him the story was dead.

"I must admit I was angry," said Gilbert. "I thought at the time and I thought even more in the years since, they don't know what they're doing. I mean, they had a chance to come out with something which was really pretty important." A year later, *Look* ran a story with studio photos of Dylan, where he wore clothes brought in for the occasion. Gilbert describes his pictures as having "rougher edges" than the slick studio shots, but what you and I are more likely to see today is the fresh intimacy and even innocence Dylan put on display in those few days. The photographer recognizes this, too: "I mean, I look at it now and I say to myself, 'Rougher edges? There are no rough edges.'"

Gilbert remembers that Dylan and Baez had come up to the **Look** offices to look over the story's layout. He found out when he ran into them on the street outside the magazine's office. They were pleased with what they'd seen, and he was pleased they'd seen it.

When he got inside, though, an editor told him the story was dead.

VII

Gilbert's shots of the country's biggest folk music festival, held in Peabody Park in the monied holiday capital of Newport, Rhode Island, couldn't change the editors' minds. In the world of *Look* magazine, the Newport Folk Festival meant very little.

In the world of folk music, Newport was the World Series.

Promoter George Wein proposed doing a Newport Folk Festival in 1959, inspired by the profitability of his annual Newport Jazz Festivals, and by the commercial folk music revival, which was nearing its peak. The first two festivals presented a very broad range of folk music, from the theatrical (Theodore Bikel) to country (Jimmie Driftwood), gospel (The Clara Ward Singers) to blues (the near-mythic Robert Pete Williams). Bluegrass banjo pioneer Earl Scruggs closed the show, after Joan Baez, presented by her early mentor, Bob Gibson, had already stolen the audience. But offstage, the music continued long into the night—as historian Robert Cantwell writes, "Newport *was* its audience." That remained true every year it was held.

After Wein's promotions were closed down due to riots at the 1960 jazz festival, a new Newport Folk Foundation formed. (The core of its board included Wein, but also Pete Seeger, Bikel, Mike Seeger, and other folkies.) It oriented the programs much more to traditional music, including country stringbands, blues, gospel, bluegrass, and other ethnic performers. During the afternoons, smaller workshops were presented for performers, songwriters, scholars, and fans of specific types of music. The Newport Festivals of 1963 through 1968 were triumphs of such programming, centered in a clear idea of the continuing life of the American folk tradition and as well-balanced as the board knew how to make them. Everyone was paid the same—the fifty dollar union minimum—from barely known Greenwich Village singer-songwriters to stars like Johnny Cash, who played there in 1964. Urban bluesmen were even allowed to use their amplifiers, although when urban folksingers tried doing the same, trouble erupted. But by 1968, even that was no problem.

Newport 1963, which featured the emergence of Dylan and the appearance of the beautiful, embattled SNCC Freedom Singers, a quartet of singing civil rights activists, and the 1965 festival, which featured Dylan's first public appearance with a rock band, are the most famous.

The festival of 1964 is the "lost" festival, without such epochal moments, but it was plenty historic in its own right. For one thing, it featured the appearance by Cash: A huge country music star aligned himself with folk, without deploring its associations with the political left and the racial integration movement. More than 70,000 people attended that year; more than 200 artists performed. "Twenty-five thousand cowboy hats, 25,000 foot-loose subway ramblers, 25,000 doe-eyed, soft focus young kids on a truth hunt—all look for Heroes to deify," wrote Paul Nelson.

Dylan plays the afternoon topical songs workshop. Visible to his right, sitting in chairs on stage, are Peter Seeger and Malvina Reynolds (who wrote "Little Boxes," among others).

In 1965, Dylan proclaimed that, "America should put statues up to The Beatles. They helped give this country's pride back to it." He also named Motown's Smokey Robinson as "America's greatest living poet."

The Newport cops tried to keep gatherings limited to the festival grounds, but groups of singing, guitar-picking, harmonica-blowing, banjo-strumming folkies swarmed into other parks, the beaches and onto the streets late into the nights. Such mass participation didn't make everyone happy: "the Newport Committee enlisted what looked to be every folk singer, or reasonable facsimile, on the North American continent. . . . Scores of traditional artists remained virtually unnoticed in the back pew," Nelson said. That trend proved irreversible. The heart of the folk music revival—which was tied in with the early '60s rediscovery of many traditional blues and mountain performers previously known only from obscure recordings—had begun to wither.

Dylan didn't cause that change, but he responded to it. That didn't mean abandoning the folk world, it meant prying it open and trying to give the music, the performers, and the ideas they represented back to the broadest possible spectrum of people. In 1965, Dylan proclaimed that, "America should put statues up to The Beatles. They helped give this country's pride back to it." He also named Motown's Smokey Robinson as "America's greatest living poet." But to the Folk Police, that was just self-promotion. They couldn't hear rock 'n' roll and rhythm and blues, soul music and the British Invasion as part of the folk music continuum even when Johnny Cash said, "It's all folk music; ain't never heard no horse singing." Why should the credentialed folklorists and experts among the Folk Police pay any attention to a guy from Dyess, Arkansas, any more than they'd really believed Big Bill Broonzy and Woody Guthrie when they said almost exactly the same thing. In reality, the contemporary music excluded from Newport represented a much clearer assessment of what was happening in the

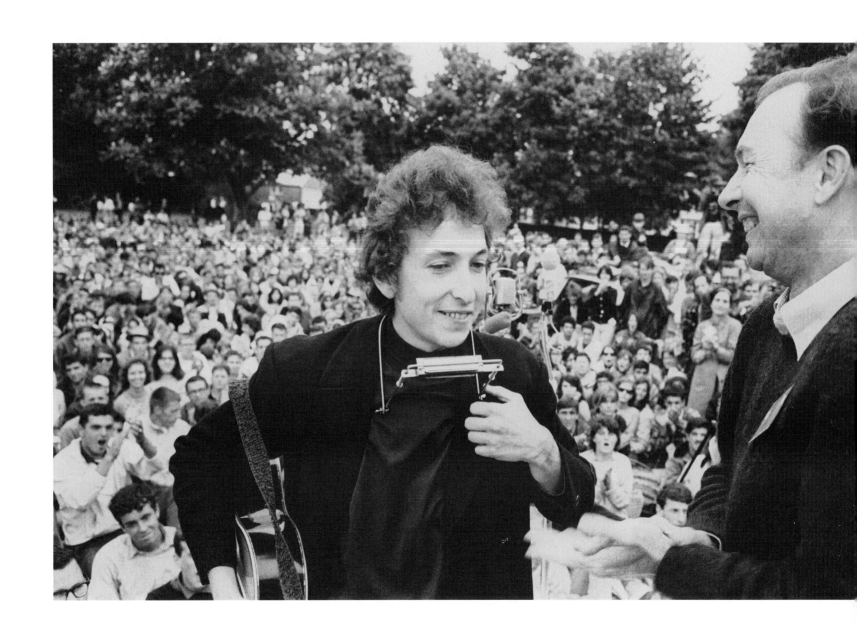

Baez and Dylan close
the 1964 Newport
Folk Festival.

"folk process" than the contemporary music included in it. Dylan was the exception, and the response to the effect such processes were having on him proved the rule.

Backstage at Newport 1964, there was indeed a much greater business presence but it didn't have a thing to do with electric instruments, love songs (without which, no blues or mountain singers could have appeared), or a lack of protest songs. Tony Glover, the harmonica player in the Minneapolis-based folk group Koerner, Ray and Glover, a brilliantly laconic wit and raconteur and one of Dylan's oldest friends in music, described the scene brilliantly in "Addendum," an essay he wrote for a 1973 songbook built around photographs by David Gahr, the Matthew Brady of the folk revival, that also featured an essay by fellow Minnesotan Paul Nelson:

That was my first glimpse of real big-time wheeling and dealing. Executives and booking agents were negotiating and hustling like berserk windmills. "I'll trade you a second act Sunday afternoon for third slot Saturday night." Grown men snarled at each other, shook hands, grinned and bickered, while the musicians stood by and watched as they were bartered like sides of beef. But what the hell, we were just in it for the music anyway.

Dylan was there that year. So was Baez. Johnny Cash and the Staple Singers, the Chambers Brothers and Robert Pete Williams. Lots of folks, lots of music. It was starting to get weird around Dylan by then. We knew him from Minnesota, used to work some of the same coffeehouses, end up at the same parties. But he was starting to be a kind of "star" in people's eyes and they would follow him in the parking lots and lobbies. (I remember one afternoon, just sitting around the hotel, he was on guitar and vocal, Bobby Neuwirth was on maracas and vocal, and I was on harp. We were doing Rolling Stones songs like "King Bee" and "Tell Me," and when we finished, from outside the door came applause. We opened the door and there were 12 or 14 people huddled in the hall. We looked at each other and wondered. . . .)

Besides this Rolling Stones jam with his pals and trading licks with Cash in Baez's room at the Viking Motor Court, Dylan appeared twice at that year's Festival. He and Baez closed the show on the final night—at that point, no one could have followed them—with their duet on "With God on Our Side," which they had been doing at her shows for months.

The performance, while greeted enthusiastically by the audience, was seen as apostasy by the Folk Police.

Before that, Dylan played a solo set featuring four songs from *Another Side* ("It Ain't Me Babe," "All I Really Want to Do," "To Ramona," and "Chimes of Freedom") plus the public debut of an unreleased song, "Mr. Tambourine Man." "Instead of all the political material everybody expected, he did songs from *Another Side* . . . like 'Ramona,'" Glover noted. "You could tell the audience was puzzled, but they didn't want to be thought *uncool* by anybody, so they applauded just as vigorously anyhow."

Dylan had performed the same material that afternoon at the Topical Songs workshop, alongside several others, including Cash, Pete Seeger, Malvina Reynolds, Jimmie Driftwood, "Tom Dooley" composer Frank Proffit, the Chad Mitchell Trio (whose pop-folk albums far outsold Dylan's), and newcomer Phil Ochs. These songs protested plenty, but not about political topics. (Unless you considered that the metaphors about the alienated psychic condition of the times were a form of political protest.) Only "Chimes of Freedom" came close to meeting the contemporary definition of "topical" and "All I Really Want to Do" and "It Ain't Me Babe" smacked of renunciation.

The performance, while greeted enthusiastically by the audience, was seen as apostasy by the Folk Police. It's worth noting that Seeger, while he had his own point of view and it wasn't rock 'n' roll, was not one of these cops. As a supremely astute judge of song quality, he knew well that Dylan's new songs were marvelous, even if they weren't about what they were supposed to be about.

To some of the enforcers of musical-political standards, Dylan just needed to be toppled from his throne. In *Broadside*, the magazine concentrated almost exclusively on political material that had printed the lyrics to many of Dylan's first songs, Paul

Wolfe announced that the festival "marked the emergence of Phil Ochs as the most important voice in the movement." Ochs had released just one album, *All the News That's Fit to Sing*, and thirteen of its fifteen tracks were "topical." Ochs had written an essay in praise of "The Lonesome Death of Hattie Carroll" in *Broadside*'s previous issue. He loved Dylan's new work and said so to everyone who asked.

Irwin Silber, editor of *Sing Out!*, decided to dethrone Dylan with a lecture, and wrote him an open letter that appeared in the magazine's November issue. Silber adopted a tone appropriate to a fairly hip father lecturing a wayward child: "You seem to be in a different kind of bag now, Bob—and I'm worried about it. I saw at Newport how you had somehow lost contact with people. It seemed to me that some of the paraphernalia of fame were getting in your way. You travel with an entourage now—with good buddies who are going to laugh when you need laughing and drink wine with you and insure your privacy—and never challenge you to face everyone else's reality again."

But Silber's real concern wasn't Dylan. It was the way his new songs veered away from being orthodox political statements: "Your new songs seem to be all inner-directed now, inner-probing, self-conscious—maybe even a little maudlin or a little cruel on occasion." Five paragraphs earlier, Silber had praised the viciously cruel "Masters of War," as well as "Blowin' in the Wind," the epitome of maudlin.

What really troubled Silber, it seemed, was not something Dylan had written but something he'd said: "You said you weren't a writer of 'protest' songs—or any other category, for that matter—but you just wrote songs. Well, okay, call it anything you want.

But any songwriter who tries to deal honestly with reality in this world is bound to write 'protest' songs. How can he help himself?"

It's hard to respond to this without amazement. The Folk Police asked only rhetorical questions, that much was obvious, but Silber had heard "It Ain't Me Babe" without hearing the protest, which surpasses expectations.

"I think, in a sense, that we are all responsible for what's been happening to you—and to many other fine young artists," Silber continued, then lowered the ideological boom. "The American Success Machinery chews up geniuses at a rate of one a day and still hungers for more. Unable to produce real art on its own, the Establishment breeds creativity in protest against and nonconformity to the System. And then, through notoriety, fast money, and status, it makes it almost impossible for the artist to function and grow."

Such rumblings were going on during the final day of the festival of course. But the weekend ended on an extremely positive note for Dylan, anyway. According to Glover, after the final concert, "in a motel room full of Joan Baez, Sandy Bull, Jack Elliott, and some others, Dylan and Cash sat on the floor trading songs. Joan set up a little portable machine and that's where Bob gave Johnny 'It Ain't Me Babe' and 'Mama, You've Been on My Mind.' Johnny was there with June Carter, so shy and sweet and gentle, in a room full of freaks. Afterward, Johnny took Bob aside and gave him his guitar—an old country gesture of admiration."

VIII

The Bob Dylan who played the '64 Newport festival was seen no more after his San Francisco appearance the night after Thanksgiving. Already songs with a rock 'n' roll beat—"If You Gotta Go, Go Now" most prominently—had begun to show up in his sets, although he remained a solo performer. In January he went into Columbia's New York studio and ended his folk period by recording "Subterranean Homesick Blues," based on a tune taken not from a spiritual but a hit record by Chuck Berry. The Folk Police behaved with predictable indignation. On his next album, *Highway 61 Revisited,* Dylan may or may not have given them the back of his hand with "Ballad of a Thin Man." In those days, his songs often displayed annoyance with pests and squares. He always remembered, though, that he was BOB DYLAN and didn't have to say anything unless he wanted to.

To those who believe that Dylan discards identities, it must be surprising how often he wants to say something. *Bringing It All Back Home* continually mixes American history and politics into the lyrics: "Bob Dylan's 115th Dream" recasts the story as a derelict's blues; the aphorisms of "Gates of Eden" and "It's All Right, Ma, I'm Only Bleeding" often take political topics; "Maggie's Farm" and "Subterranean Homesick Blues" can be used as sage, if cryptic, guide-books for outlaws and revolutionaries. (Whether they guide in wise directions remains up to the user.)

Dylan didn't return to writing specifically "topical" songs, torn from recent headlines (as opposed to the yellowed ones of "John Wesley Harding"), until 1971, when he put out a single called "George Jackson." Jackson was a petty thief given a life sentence in the California prison system for a $70 gas station robbery. While there, he educated himself and became a black nationalist intellectual and a best-selling author. On August 21, 1971, prison guards gunned him down in the San Quentin yard; his body was found holding a pistol, and the shooting was written off as a jailbreak.

Dylan's song reflected more knowledge of the facts of Jackson's legal case than it did reading of *Letters from Soledad*. Dylan wasn't writing about a literary figure or even an ordinary victim of the legal and penal systems. "George Jackson" returned him to a central political concern: freedom for black Americans.

Mainly, "George Jackson" deals with Dylan's central ethical concern: The need for liberty, justice, and equality as a precondition for full humanity. It is an expression of the idea that the quest for the realization of these things is the responsibility of every individual. This is an idea found in "Like a Rolling Stone" every bit as much as "The Lonesome Death of Hattie Carroll." Dylan didn't entirely abandon the theme even during his period of writing Christian evangelistic songs in the late 1970s and early 1980s. "People starving and thirsting, grain elevators are bursting / Oh, you know it costs more to store the food than it do to give it," Dylan wrote in "You Gotta Serve Somebody." In the masterpiece of his evangelical period, "Every Grain of Sand," he writes, "Like Cain, I now behold this chain of events that I must break," which is nothing that wouldn't fit alongside "When the Ship Comes In" or for that matter, "Blowin' in the Wind."

He said it best at the time in "I Shall Be Free No. 10," in one of the few lines there that might not be entirely a celebration of the put-on: "Now I'm liberal, but to a degree / I want everybody to be free."

It's serious partly because it's a set up for the next couplet, about Barry Goldwater not being allowed to live in his neighborhood or join his family, but mostly because it's the follow-up to Dylan's showstopper at the Tom Paine award ceremony, and the prelude to everything he'd say from "Maggie's Farm" to "Sugar Baby," the concluding song on *Love and Theft,* his album released on September 11, 2001: "I got my back to the sun 'cause the light is too intense / I can see what everybody in the world is up against."

IX

When Newport ended, Douglas Gilbert vanished from Bob Dylan's world. He seemed unlikely ever to return. Because *Look* never ran the story, almost nobody knew the pictures he'd made even existed. The negatives returned to his files in 1971, when *Look* folded. Gilbert told his family about them, but uncertain of who really owned the publication rights he never pursued using them. Anyway, he was busy with other projects, including the book *C. S. Lewis: Images of His World,* architectural photography, and teaching. Beginning in the 1990s, he went back to school and became a clinical social worker practicing psychotherapy. (Wouldn't the kind of close and intelligent observer who made these photographs make a good therapist?) Since 1994, he's devoted himself full-time to photographic projects.

In 2004, Douglas found out for sure that he owned the Dylan photographs. The Perfect Exposure Gallery in Los Angeles presented an exhibition of forty-two of them as "Bob Dylan: Unscripted" in February 2005.

This timing was perfect. Columbia planned to release *The Bootleg Series Vol. 6: Bob Dylan Live 1964, Concert at Philharmonic Hall,* from a show he did that Halloween. The first of Douglas Gilbert's pictures were published in the album's accompanying booklet. Around the same time, Martin Scorsese was finishing *No Direction Home*, a documentary film about Dylan's life, and more of the pictures appear in both the film and in the packaging of its soundtrack album.

Dylan had never seen the pictures. He loved them, according to his art director Geoff Gans. "One of the things Bob really liked is you can see the furniture, which to him really dates the time. He also liked the photos of him sitting around with a bunch of people because they weren't just focused on him," Gans told the *Boston Globe.*

For the Perfect Exposure exhibition, a catalog was created, featuring an extensive interview with Douglas Gilbert, conducted by his daughter Rachel, who had urged him to pursue the Dylan project. (Most of the quotations from the photographer in this book are from that interview.)

At its conclusion, Douglas reflects on the entire encounter with Dylan.

"When I began listening to him as a college student, I realized that this guy was writing and saying things in songs that I hadn't put words to. But when he was singing them I said, 'Yes, of course, that's really important, that's what puts words to the feelings that I've had. . . .' And what he was doing was really writing and explaining, as well as artic-ulating, what was percolating in my own mind but I didn't have the words for. . . . [He] began to put some form in my own thinking that I could connect with. And I said I really identify with this guy and—how does he do this? I was amazed. Nobody was writing like he was. It was petty shocking early on and I think a lot of people didn't know what to do with him because we hadn't had experience with this kind of stuff. But, to me, it was just a powerful connection."

Many Dylan fans felt such a sense of connection. The trick is to do something with it. Douglas Gilbert didn't waste his chance. The pictures he made, unjustly withheld for so many years, confront each of us with the same challenge. In that respect, the beauty of *Forever Young* not only celebrates history, but also confronts the present and the future. Now, the opportunity is ours.